THE

MITHRAIC

RITE

ARYA AETERNA

Book I

THE
MITHRAIC RITE

Arya Aeterna Book I

Published by Sanctus Arya Press

First edition, published in June of 2025 by Sanctus Arya Press.

This work is copyrighted © 2025 by Ordo Arya Aeterna.

Paperback: 978-1-968394-00-4

Hardcover: 978-1-968394-01-1

Library of Congress Number pending.

Cover art, editing, and layout by Frater Sigma.

Inside illustrations taken from the public domain.

More at:

aryaaeterna.com

sanctusarya.com

This volume was crafted by anonymous initiates in service to the Great Work and furthering a Northern Esoteric Tradition of Perennial Wisdom.

PER VIRTUTEM

PER IGNEM

PER MITHRAM

SURGO

("By virtue, by fire, by Mithras — I rise.")

Table of Contents

Introduction

We live in the twilight of the West. This is an age of dissolution where sacrality has been replaced by the profane, and quality by the common. Yet, the initiatory Mithraic current remains alive for those who venture to awaken it.

This treatise is not an academic exercise. It is a manual for action, synthesizing the wisdom of the Radical Traditionalist school into a Mithraic approach to present-day spiritual warfare.

Drawing from esoteric exegesis, structural analysis of initiation, reconstruction of Mithraic liturgy, metaphysics of sacred science, and an overall Indo-European framework, we shall forge a rite — not a mere imitation of antiquity, but an adaptation for a contemporary aspirant among the ruins. Mithraism is a mystery tradition, meaning its truths are not just grasped intellectually, but lived.

This exploration of Mithraism is a call to reactivate an ancient virile spirituality in the modern wasteland. Unlike exoteric religions demanding passive belief, this is a path of action: ritual, ordeal, and shaping an unbreakable will. For the seeker navigating the ruins of a decadent age, this is a way to transcend the materialist prison of modernity through the Solar Warrior ethos of Mithras.

The Mithraic Mysteries

The Mithraic Mysteries form one of the most profound religious complexes of the ancient world — a sacred tradition veiled in secrecy yet permeating substance. Though the outer forms of Mithraism vanished with the triumph of Christianity, its core truths, rites of inner transformation, and archetypal motifs remain accessible to the serious seeker.

Mithraism flourished in the Roman Empire between the 1st and 4th centuries CE. It was a mystery cult centered around the god Mithras, often depicted within subterranean sanctuaries in the act of slaying a bull (the *Tauroctony*). These spaces were not temples in the public sense, but sacred caves in which initiates journeyed from ignorance to illumination.

The cult was exclusively male. It inducted members through a series of seven degrees, each symbolizing a spiritual and cosmological ascent.

Far from being a mere exotic religious sect, the Mithraic Mysteries conveyed a rigorous initiatory path. Mithraism was not a religion in the modern sense of sentiment or belief, but a "regality of the soul" enacted through ordeal, transformation, and conquest — not chiefly of others, but oneself.

The symbolism of the Tauroctony is central. Mithras slays the bull, and from this act the cosmos is born: wheat sprouts from its tail, a scorpion bites its testicles (symbolizing degeneration or entropic decay), and celestial signs frame the image. The act is not a moral narrative but a cosmogenic, timeless gesture — a representation of transcending chaos, harnessing vital energy, and orienting one's life toward eternal order.

Mithras did not emerge *ex nihilo* in the Roman period. His line traces back through Indo-European tradition, manifesting differently across cultures. In Vedic India, Mitrá is god of oaths, order, and friendship.

He is one half of the divine dyad Mitrá–Varuṇa. While Mitrá maintains the world's contracts and stability, Varuṇa enforces them with the binding power of magic and appraisal. The balance of juridical authority (mitraic) and mystical dominion (varunic) is a core duality within Indo-European sovereignty.

In Iranian culture, Mithra (Miθra) evolves as a deity of light, loyalty, and war. He is venerated in the Avesta. Zoroastrianism assimilated but relegated him to a secondary role beneath Ahura Mazda.

Nevertheless, his solar and warrior aspects endured. It is from this Iranian foundation Roman Mithraism likely drew its spiritual DNA. Although the Roman form of the cult radically transformed this inheritance through Hellenistic overlays.

Mithras represents the cosmic force capable of moving the equinoxial precession, unlocking a cosmological function far

12

beyond mere solar symbolism. In this light, he becomes a metaphysical principle: conqueror of fate, time, and cyclical existence. A spiritual liberator to one who escapes the world of appearances.

The Mithraic grades — Corax ("*Raven*"), Nymphus ("*Bridegroom*"), Miles ("*Soldier*"), Leo ("*Lion*"), Perses ("*Persian*"), Heliodromus ("*Sun-Runner*"), and Pater ("*Father*") — constitute an ascending order of spiritual maturity and cosmic correspondence. Each rank reflects a celestial body, an archetypal quality, and a stage of existential purification.

For instance, Miles represents disciplined courage, the readiness to fight — not just in the world, but the self, against spiritual inertia. The Leo stage brings fire and assertive vitality, while Heliodromus is a Solar Hero: one who follows the sun's course toward immortality. The final stage, Pater, is the embodiment of Mithraic wisdom and cosmic authority: a microcosmic sovereign embodying divine order.

This initiatory ascent is mirrored in the *philosophia perennis*: universal wisdom Rene Guénon called a Primordial Tradition. Through ritual, ordeal, and contemplation, the Mithraic initiate overcame the merely human and actualized transcendence, the vertical axis of being. Such rites serve as a symbolic death and rebirth — a means to exit profane time and participate in a sacred, timeless reality.

The key to Mithraism is not mere belief, but praxis. It is a way of being, not simply a theology. It is through the ritual reenactment of cosmic truths — within the cave, under firelight, before the Tauroctony — one aligns with the solar essence of Mithras Sol Invictus, who neither submits to matter nor chaos.

Though Mithraism was officially suppressed under Christian emperors in the fourth century CE, its symbols and ethos did not vanish. Some scholars trace elements of Mithraism into early Christianity — not dogmatic content, but symbolic continuity. Iconography of a dying and rising god, the sacred meal, and the cave-nativity (as seen in Nativity traditions) suggest an overlay of Mithraic ritual memory upon Christian liturgy.

Furthermore, in the realm of esotericism, certain Mithraic motifs echo within Freemasonry, Rosicrucianism, and other initiatory orders. The emphasis on secrecy, degrees of advancement, symbolic death and rebirth, and solar-astral metaphors within Masonic ritual suggest a possible inheritance or parallel evolution of initiatory forms.

Even more subtly, the Mithraic worldview lives on in those who affirm the soul's sovereignty. Those who reject the passive drift of materialism. Those who, like Evola's "differentiated man," seek mastery amidst regression.

To engage with Mithraism today is not to reenact dead rituals but to reclaim an orientation. The cave is within. The bull is one's own base nature, vital yet untamed. The dagger is not for blood but for sacrifice — the conscious severing of the lower self. Fire is both illumination and ordeal, the divine spark carried through night.

In a Mithraic context, the initiate accepts that civilization may falter and empires dissolve, but our inner domain — the

Spiritual Imperium — stands invincible, inviolable, invictus, if one lives as Mithras does: with will, clarity, and command.

The modern Mithraist need not adopt ancient costumes or imitate extinct customs. Rather, he should acquire its essence: the cosmology of ascent, ethics of solar courage, metaphysics of transformation. He must live as one aligned with the Axis Mundi, the center that is unmoved by time's decay.

The world of the masses runs horizontally, obsessed with time, sensation, distraction. The Mithraic path runs vertically into the heights of soul and depths of being. It is not for all, as it demands everything. But for those who dare wield the dagger, don the crown of sovereignty, and dwell within the cave — Mithras stands ready to guide.

The Mithraic Triune

The figure of Mithras (also Mithra or Mitrá) looms as a potent symbol of sovereignty, contract, and transcendent light throughout the ancient world. Across three great Indo-European traditions — Vedic, Zoroastrian, and Roman — he manifests in forms that share names and certain themes, yet diverge in theology, cosmology, and cultic practice. Understanding these allows for a more precise comprehension of Roman Mithraism not as the simple inheritance of an Iranian god, but an inspired and initiatic invocation of a perennial archetype.

In the ancient Rigvedic hymns of India, Mitrá appears most often paired with Varuṇa. Together, these deities represent cosmic order (Ṛta) and the ethical-spiritual dimension of the Divine Law. Mitrá in particular personifies camaraderie, pact, and social unity. He is a deity of light and scrutiny, guarantor of oaths and ties that bind society and cosmos.

Mitrá is associated with dawn — a liminal time of passage and illumination — and shares in the solar imagery common to many Indo-European sky deities. Yet he is not the actual sun; rather, he symbolizes the clarity and order radiating from solar consciousness. His role is juridical: he observes, binds, affirms, and punishes when cosmic law is violated.

Unlike Roman Mithras, Mitrá was not the focal point of an initiatory cult. However, his qualities inform an archetype of *Solar Contract-Bearer* found in Iranian and Roman contexts.

In ancient Iran, Mithra takes on a more formalized and personified role. Found in the Avesta, Mithra is again god of contracts, truth (*Asha*), and cosmic vigilance. He is described as possessing a thousand ears and ten thousand eyes, surveying the world for transgressions against divine order. He rides a chariot drawn by white horses, cuts down evil-doers, and preserves justice in a struggle between order and chaos (*druj*).

Zoroastrian Mithra becomes more militant than his Vedic counterpart — now clearly solar in character, associated with the midday sun and light as principle of truth. He is a warrior against darkness; not supreme (Ahura Mazda holds that role), but a powerful combatant in cosmic battle.

What distinguishes Iranian Mithra is this dualism: he exists in a moral universe of good versus evil. Likewise, his role is both judicial and martial. This lends itself well to a reinterpretation of the god not simply as typifying divine justice, but initiatory combat. This latter theme takes root in Roman Mithraism.

Roman Mithras — as venerated from the 1st to 4th centuries CE in underground Mithraea from Britain to Syria — is neither a crude adoption of an Iranian god nor shallow rebranding of a Greek divinity (e.g., Perseus). He is linked by name and imagery to Iranian Mithra, yet radically transformed into a figure of initiatic ascent and coupled to arcane stellar knowledge.

The central image of Mithras slaying the bull (Tauroctony) is not found in the Vedas or the Avesta. This iconography is a Roman creation layered with cosmological significance. Mithras was understood by initiates as a cosmic being who created the world by slaying a bull: a life-force that, once sacrificed, released the zodiac, moon, sun, and cycles of existence.

Here, Mithras is a solar god of transcendent action — not simply the sun, but a heroic force behind the sun. He partakes in the solar essence but is distinct from Sol Invictus, with whom he is often depicted in sacred embrace or handshake. His role is initiatory: he slays, transforms, rises.

The three forms of Mithra share essential attributes, but their functions and cultic expressions vary. While a name threads these traditions together, the Roman form is most radically interiorized and initiatory. This is not a public or state cult, but an underground school of enlightenment rooted in cosmic myth and realized through personal exaltation.

For modern seekers of the sacred and initiatory, Roman Mithras holds a unique position. He is not merely the god of justice or contracts, but archetype of heroic becoming. His rites reenact sacrifice not for pious obedience, but spiritual ascent.

The twelve zodiac signs surrounding the Tauroctony reverberate the soul's descent and return through the spheres, and torchbearers Cautes and Cautopates represent the dual principles: life and death, light and shadow, rising and setting. The bull embodies a primal force subdued by the spiritual hero who does not destroy nature, but transforms it.

Roman Mithraism proposes a spiritual physics: through stages of trial and discipline, one may rise above fate and partake in the freedom of the divine. Formerly confined to time and generation, the soul aligns with an abiding cosmic order.

The Mithraic triune (Indian, Iranian, Roman) reveals an archetype evolving across lands and epochs. In each, we find a vision of sacred order, truth, and transcendence. In Roman form, this vision becomes an initiatory path, inviting one not only to worship but to personify the god — to become Mithras.

This is not a religion of comfort, moralism, or obedience. It is a way of ascent through discipline (*disciplina*) and virility (*virtus*). The Mithraic initiate learns to wield the sword not just against men, but inner turmoil. To slay the bull of brute vitality and ride a chariot of stars toward an eternal light.

In this, Roman Mithras offers more than a forgotten mystery. He offers a starry map for those still sifting among the ruins for that eternal fire of the gods.

Mithras and the Indo-European Framework

The Mithraic Mysteries, like many ancient spiritual systems, are built upon foundations of deep symbolic meaning that span time, geography, and culture. Among the most important elements of Mithraic thought is its connection to the ancient Indo-European framework. Mithras, as a central figure in this spiritual tradition, embodies the core values of cosmic order, authority, and a martial ethos.

Mithras represents the warrior, protector of sovereignty, and enforcer of celestial stability. Within a cosmological framework he is linked to solar and astral representations clarifying his role in restoring order to a chaotic world. Mithras is not only a warrior, but also enforcer of Divine Law: someone who actively combats chaos and brings about spiritual renewal.

These ancient principles should be integrated into an immanent context in contemporary Mithraic practice. Guided by Mithras, the aspirant must learn to balance two core aspects: discipline and transcendence. The operative can through this integration embody Mithras' dual aspects, walking a path both spiritual and sensible — attuned to the twofold reality of life.

Mithras is aligned with a martial aspect, embodying the ideal of an enforcer of cosmic order. The warrior is not simply a fighter in the physical sense. He is protector of stability and law, ensuring a balance between divine and human is maintained.

Mithras in his role as bull-slayer brings order out of disorder by channeling and directing cosmic energies. He is a fighter against forces of chaos. His battle is not only one fought in the material realm; it is also a spiritual struggle against ignorance, aberration, and base impulses.

The warrior's function is essential to maintaining not just earthly order, but the very fabric of material existence. In Mithras' case, his role as warrior is linked to the sun's rising, symbolizing diurnal restoration of light and order. This daily renewal encapsulated by solar imagery speaks to Mithras' ability to uphold and reinstate dominion.

Pairing Mitrá with Varuṇa highlights the dual nature of sovereignty within Indo-European thought. While Mitrá enforces cosmic law and is a figure of discipline, Varuṇa represents the mysterious, transcendent force behind cosmic order. Mitrá aligns closely with the practical enforcement of rules while Varuṇa represents an ineffable power concealed in existence.

In Roman Mithraic tradition, this duality is evident: Mithras is simultaneously a warrior and sage. As a figure of law and sovereignty, he embodies the clarity of Mitrá's (Mithras') discipline, but as a god linked to transcendence, he also carries the principle of Varuṇa's cosmic mystery. The Mithraic aspirant must integrate worldly discipline with celestial superiority.

Mitrá calls the initiate to live in accordance with Divine Law, not simply as a set of external rules, but an inner discipline. This manifests through daily practice: purification, fasting, and focused action. The initiate must be lively, dedicated to personal growth, unwavering in their commitment to cosmic order.

Varuṇa on the other hand invites one to look beyond the material world into deeper mysteries of existence. To invoke Varuṇa is to embrace numinous aspects of the undertaking, connecting with forces beyond our immediate comprehension governing the universe. This aspect requires humbling the lower self before a greater Will.

The balance between these two forces — active discipline of Mitrá and rarefied mystery of Varuṇa — produces a congruous route for the aspirant. Without Mitrá's restraint, one might fall into passivity or self-indulgence, losing sight of the effort required for self-mastery. Without Varuṇa's eminence, one may become too focused on material concerns, missing the purpose of what is ultimately spiritual endeavor.

Mithras himself serves as archetype of this balance. His mythic journey exemplifies the union of control and sanctity. The slaying of the bull represents not just an act of physical violence, but metaphysical transformation. Mithras does not fight the bull for personal glory; he does so to restore cosmic order, ensuring that light and truth continue to prevail. The bull — often interpreted as a symbol of chaos or the untamed forces of nature — must be slain for existence to thrive.

But the bull is not merely killed in a physical sense. It is a cosmic act of sacrifice wherein Mithras channels forces of destructive transformation in creating new life. The image of Mithras atop the bull is one of victory and rebirth — a triumph over forces seeking to keep sentience imprisoned in ignorance, carnality, and materialism.

Through this act, Mithras becomes both warrior and priest. He uses disciplined power to confront and conquer the chaos of the world, but does so with an awareness of deeper, more mysterious energies at play. This balance between strength and transcendence is essential to Mithras' role in this traditional form. It also provides the present-day aspirant a structure for an esoteric spiritual practice.

For the contemporary Mithraic initiate, the principle of Mitrá's discipline translates into a daily practice of order and self-mastery. Just as Mithras is enforcer of cosmic law, the initiate must become a guardian of their own personal rules, values, and boundaries.

Train the body, maintain health, and cultivate strength — both in a physical and metaphysical sense. The aspirant should engage in routine exercises that enhance physiological vigor, fitness, and endurance. One's form is the vessel through which spiritual energy flows, and ought to embody an ideal.

Establish habits in devotion to personal growth as part of a spiritual program. The aspirant must pledge to this enterprise with the same ardor a warrior commits to battle.

Discipline is also about cultivating inner order. The initiate must take responsibility for their interior world: cutting through distractions, controlling impulses, and resisting temptations. This can be done through focused mental and emotional work, particularly practices of self-reflection and purification.

The Mithraic aspirant must see himself as a spiritual warrior battling against the forces of chaos. In a personal sense they must make war on weakness, whether that be laziness, distraction, ignorance, or self-deception.

While Mitrá represents the enforcement of cosmic law, Varuṇa represents deeper, unknowable mysteries of existence. The initiate must engage with Varuṇa's transcendent nature. In a world dominated by noise and distraction, one must retreat into quiet to hear truths existing beyond ordinary perception.

The Solar Warrior

Within the context of spiritual existence *among the ruins*, where traditional values have crumbled and the contemporary world is defined by materialism, dissolution, and nihilism, there arises a call to rediscover and reintegrate a form of transcendent spirituality. This call is captured in the ethos of the *Solar Warrior* — a term derived from the teachings of Julius Evola.

The Solar Warrior is an archetype of spiritual combat who through active participation in a higher order resists the modern world's decay and entropy. He is one who stands resolute against forces seeking to reduce man to a mere *"human animal."*

Central to this ethos is the figure of Mithras Sol Invictus ("*Unconquered Sun*"), a transcendent Apollonian force capable of overcoming death and rebirth, the cycle of time, and dark powers working to diminish existence. Mithras is not a passive figure; he is a fighter, a warrior engaged in a cosmic battle. The Solar Warrior ethos is a mindset of action, not belief.

Deeply immersed in history, metaphysics, and mythology, Evola presented a similar character in one who resists modern degradation through fortitude and a personal commitment to higher principles. In his framework, one should not be bound by worldly attachments or petty morality, but a champion of superior values based in a spiritual understanding of nobility.

Evola contrasts this "aristocrat of the soul" with a modern man who is above all effete and passive: caught in the throes of decadent materialism and subject to the whims of collective opinion. He urged for one to stand against this passive existence and transcend mass society. Evola's ideal is one of active resistance to adversaries both inner and outer.

The Solar Warrior ethos requires adopting the spirit of a *miles* ("*soldier*") willing to endure hardships, challenges, even defeat, all while remaining committed to transcendent values. The predominate battleground is not material, but spiritual — it is a fight against entropic forces pulling one into a downward spiral of ignorance and diminished existence. This war takes discipline, durability, and courage; it requires unwavering resilience, a commitment to quality, and devotion to an ideal.

René Guénon, foremost proponent of Traditionalist thought, viewed the decline of modern society as a symptom of a deeper spiritual malaise: the loss of connection with a higher, timeless order. In his works, Guénon speaks of a golden age of those who lived in accord with divine principles governing the cosmos.

For him, the majority of people had become disconnected from higher levels of existence, leading them to live in a state of degeneration. A key task is in reviving this association through disciplined study, accurate insight, and appropriate practice.

Guénon's traditionalist ideal emphasizes the importance of living in accordance with sacred rites and practices. It also highlights the necessity to confront modernity's deepening spiritual crisis. The Solar Warrior must fight with dignity, resolve, and courage against a world in which the sacred is all but defeated — he must keep the holy fire in this darkest hour.

Georges Dumézil, a scholar of ancient mythology, provides additional insight into this ethos by examining the role of the warrior within Indo-European cultures. His work on the trifunctional hypothesis posits these societies were organized around three functions: the laborer, the priest, and the warrior.

The warrior function, as articulated by Dumézil, embodies the concept of force in protecting and defending order. In many Indo-European traditions, the warrior was associated with solar deities such as Mithras, who represents the unyielding light of truth and justice. The Solar Warrior is an archetype of active engagement with the world — he is one whose energy and force are directed toward the preservation of the divine order.

The Solar Warrior's role is not primarily contemplative. He is actively engaged in confronting chaos and darkness, possessing both physical prowess and psychic tenacity. Dumézil's analysis underscores the importance of a warrior's role within society and connection to the sacred, showing he is more than a combatant — he is a vessel of cosmic order and guardian of sacrality.

In the context of contemporary spiritual existence, particularly in an age defined by the ruins of traditional structures, how can one embody the Solar Warrior ethos practically? How can the modern initiate live as a warrior against the forces of entropy, materialism, and decadence?

The first step for the present-day Solar Warrior is to reject the passive stance of the modern world. In a society dominated by consumerism, entertainment, and the pursuit of individual pleasure, the warrior must turn away from these distractions and engage in active resistance against the forces that keep him bound to materiality.

This resistance is not merely intellectual or emotional; it is a lifestyle. The warrior must practice discipline, structure, and focus in all aspects of his life. This includes cultivating physical strength and health, as the body is the vessel for spiritual power, but also dedicating time to intellectual and spiritual development. A Solar Warrior does not simply think about the world and its spiritual decay — he acts to transform himself and his environment. He lives the teachings, engages in practice, and strives to create order amidst chaos.

The combat of the Solar Warrior is not external but internal. The greatest battle the warrior faces is against his own lower impulses, his desires, and his attachments to the world. To engage in this combat, the initiate must cultivate inner stillness, focus, and impartiality. Meditation, self-reflection, and a consistent practice of ritual and prayer can serve as the tools of the Solar Warrior in his inner battle.

The Solar Warrior must face his fears, his doubts, and his weaknesses with the same determination that he would face a physical enemy. This requires constant vigilance and a refusal to succumb to the distractions and temptations of modern life. Like a soldier training for battle, the warrior must develop habits that increase his steadfastness and prepare him for the struggles ahead.

Reconnecting with tradition is essential. This can be done through study of traditional texts, practicing sacred rituals, and cultivation of a mindset prioritizing the sacred over the profane. Initiation into a formal esoteric order can serve as a means of grounding the initiate in a higher, transcendent purpose.

While traditional societies provided structured paths to follow, the modern world lacks adequate institutions. However, the contemporary Solar Warrior can find his path through personal commitment to spiritual growth, association with like-minded individuals, and participation in the ongoing battle for the soul. This war is fought not through outward action alone, but internal transformation and a commitment to living in accordance with Divine Law.

The Solar Warrior ethos offers a powerful framework for contemporary spiritual existence in an age marked by decay and crisis. In the face of crumbling edifice, he stands as a beacon of transcendent action, discipline, and resilience.

Occult War

In a time when corruption, excess, and absurdity prevail, the concept of *Occult War* emerges as an elemental context to understand a metaphysical battle shaping our world. This war transcends physical conflicts, delving into the spiritual and ideological realms where Tradition faces relentless subversion. For the Mithraic initiate, this war is not merely an external phenomenon, but an internal journey towards self-realization and cosmic alignment.

Julius Evola posits in *Men Among the Ruins* that the crises dominating modern civilization are manifestations of a hidden war aimed at dismantling spiritual values and reducing man to the docile instrument of a seditious kleptocracy. This conflict is not fought with conventional or even high-tech weapons but through manipulating ideology, shifting culture, and eroding traditional institutions — all using age-old occult means.

In *The Occult & Subversive Movements*, Bolton expands on this by examining the role of occult groups and doctrines in fomenting revolutions and undermining traditional spirituality to establish a one-world syncretic religion. He highlights the use of materialistic, rationalistic, and communistic ideologies (often seeming against esotericism) as tools of this subversive agenda.

To navigate the complexities of Occult War, it's essential to distinguish between "anti-Tradition" and "counter-Tradition." Anti-Tradition represents a direct opposition to traditional values, often manifesting as secularism, materialism, and the rejection of spiritual hierarchies. It seeks to dismantle the structures that uphold sacred order.

Counter-Tradition is more insidious, as it mimics traditional forms while subverting their essence. This introduces distorted spiritualities and pseudo-religions leading seekers astray, away from true transcendence. Understanding this distinction is crucial for the Mithraic aspirant, who must discern genuine paths of enlightenment from deceptive imitations.

The Occult War's roots trace back to ancient times, but its modern manifestations became prominent during the Enlightenment, which emphasized reason over faith leading to the marginalization of spiritual traditions. The French Revolution further accelerated this decline by dismantling the monarchy and the Church's authority, replacing them with secular institutions.

In the 20th century, communist and ostensibly democratic regimes exploited occult symbols and teachings, distorting their meanings for political ends. Today the war continues through globalist machinations combined with the proliferation of ideologies that erode cultural and spiritual identities.

Faced with this Occult War, the Mithraic initiate adopts the role of Solar Warrior, embodying virtues counteracting forces of decay. Through them, one not only resists the subversive currents of Occult War, but also becomes a beacon of Tradition, inspiring others to seek the superior.

The Occult War challenges the very foundations of spiritual existence, seeking to sever humanity's connection to the transcendent. Yet, through the path of Mithras one can rise above, embodying an eternal warrior who upholds sacred order. In embracing this role one not only safeguards their self, but contributes to the restoration of a world aligned with Divine Law.

The Occult War is an invisible yet all-pervasive conflict — waged with ideas, symbols, norms, and energies. It is fought in the interior planes, manifesting through cultural ideologies, social systems, and spiritual currents. In this war, the enemy is not merely modernity or secularism, but a deeper process of de-sacralization, aimed at dismantling the sacred order embedded in the cosmos: the Primordial Tradition that once integrated political, religious, and social into an organic unity.

Guénon especially emphasized the existence of an anti-initiatic center operating through false esoteric movements, giving rise to distorted influences masquerading as "universal wisdom." The Occult War in the 20th and 21st centuries has evolved through new channels. New Age movements are part of the spiritual entropy of the age. They simulate forms of ancient wisdom but lack initiation, doctrine, and ascesis. They claim insight and authority, but at best are sentimental mystics.

The fusion of democratic egalitarianism with esoteric language promises mass awakening, planetary ascension, and "unity consciousness," all of which upturn the hierarchical nature of reality. This signifies a triumph of Counter-Tradition: a leveling of the sacred, when it is innately aristocratic.

The modern world is a battlefield on which a terminal stage of Occult War is being waged. The digital era presents an illusion of knowledge, experiences are reduced to neurochemistry, real interaction is replaced by social media, and the masses believe themselves "awake" while their slumber deepens. They are further stifled by horizontal, materialistic pseudo-mythologies (e.g., simulation theory, AI as godhead, aliens as deities, etc.).

In Guénon's metaphysical terms, we are surrounded not by men of spirit but golems animated by ideologies, consumption, and automation. Evola saw this as a realization of the "*subhuman*" — an inversion of spiritual hierarchy. Techno-Gnosticism (a transhumanist phantasmagoria of immortality, consciousness uploading, and synthetic nirvana) is the final parody of initiation. It replaces spiritual ascent with mechanized apotheosis: a titanic revolt against heaven.

To live as a Solar Warrior in the midst of Occult War is to follow the way of Mithras slaying the bull. It is the conquest of lower, chaotic energies by a virile force of spiritual will.

What does this mean practically? The aspirant must study patterns of inversion — not obsess over them, but become immune to their influence. One does not fight shadows with shadows, but solar clarity. Like the Roman *contubernia*, small groups may gather to fortify themselves through rite, study, and discipline. These are not clubs, but sovereign cells of resistance in a metaphysical war.

The first battlefield is the self. Evola emphasized that before one confronts the enemy without, one must fortify the citadel within. This is done through ascesis (spiritual discipline), knowledge (discerning true from false initiation), and ritual (realigning with the Primordial Tradition).

To stand as a pillar between heaven and earth, as Mithras does, is to become Axis Mundi. In a world of horizontalism where all is leveled, one must reassert the vertical: spirit over matter, order over chaos, sovereignty over dissolution.

The Occult War is not a conspiracy in the profane sense. It is a metaphysical reality: the struggle of titans against Olympians, an uprising of matter against spirit. It is not a war that can be "won" in time, for time and space are battlegrounds.

To the Solar Warrior, the task is not to save the world, but to stand in it undefeated. It is to embody the solar principle, pass through ordeal, and affect others by example. For Mithras lives in the deed.

The bull is slain anew each day.

The sun rises after the darkest night.

The Roman Style

"The perfection of the human being is the end to which every healthy social institution must be subordinated... This perfection must be conceived on the basis of a process of individuation and progressive differentiation." —Julius Evola

This age is marked by egalitarian leveling, consumerist narcotics, and terminal confusion. In such times, invoking the Roman Style is not wistfulness. It is an act of spiritual rebellion: a restoration of form versus amorphousness, hierarchy against chaos, and virile soul opposing bureaucratic emptiness.

The Roman Style is not merely a cultural aesthetic or historical memory. It is a metaphysical code; an ethos that shapes the soul into a vehicle of transcendence. It is the terrestrial armature for those striving toward the vertical axis and Absolute Principle — the Flame of Mithras.

For the Traditionalist aspirant, a Roman Style is more than a guide — it is a discipline of being and daily practice in thought, discourse, and action. It embodies the same sacred orientation that animated patrician and legionnaire alike: an aristocracy of soul, where action is deliberate, spirit is forged in fire, and divinity is honored not with sentiment, but strength.

Let us then enumerate and reawaken these virtues, not as dead concepts, but as living pillars in constructing the heroic individual.

Virtus — Virile Spirit and Solar Courage

Virtus is not morality. It is not obedience, nor sentimentality. It is courage imbued with metaphysical fire, not simply to act, but affirm oneself against dissolution. For the Mithraic warrior virtus is a dagger raised in sacred revolt — against fear, fate, and mollifying influence of modernity.

Practically: Rise at dawn to salute the Sun. Engage in physical rigor, abstaining from indulgence. Speak with clarity, not passion; choose stillness over noise and action over protest.

Fortitudo and Constantia — Spiritual Strength and Inner Constancy

This is the firmness of a mountain amid storms: the ability to withstand, to persist, to hold one's center even when all forms crumble around you. It is Evola's *"riding the tiger"* — not giving in to the world's current, but remaining unmoved, inviolable, sovereign.

Practically: Maintain a consistent spiritual regimen. Rise and retire at fixed hours. Do not yield to emotional fluctuations. Hold your silence when provoked. Endure pain without lament.

Sapientia — Thoughtful Awareness and Active Knowledge

Not intellectualism, but intuitive wisdom. The ability to perceive the structure of reality, to discern illusion from essence. *Sapientia* is what orients an initiate to the Primordial Tradition, enabling him to decode symbols, rites, and cosmic laws.

Practically: Study traditional metaphysics — Guénon, Evola, the Indo-European spiritual canon. Contemplate; do not seek to "know more," but to know deeply. Maintain a sacred journal. Observe the world as signs, not objects.

Disciplina — Form and the Law Given by the Self

Discipline is not punishment. It is form, voluntarily accepted, shaping chaos into cosmos. The initiate imposes order upon his life as the Romans imposed order upon their provinces: not to control, but to elevate.

Practically: Keep your quarters in strict order. Master your appetites. Avoid glaring at screens and read more. Obey your own law with greater severity than any imposed from without.

Fides — Loyalty and Sacred Trust

Not belief, but trust rooted in fidelity to one's word, one's path, one's gods. The Mithraic initiate must embody solar loyalty — to his brotherhood, the divine, and his sacred vow.

Practically: Do not speak what you cannot live; promise only what you can fulfill. Be steadfast in duties to self and kin.

Dignitas, Gravitas, Solemnitas — Weight of Being and Sovereign Composure

Dignity is not pride — it is the radiance of inner authority. Gravitas is the spiritual weight that turns attention into presence. Solemnitas is not somberness, but the sacred tone with which one approaches life.

Practically: Move slowly and with intention. Avoid loudness, vulgarity, and excess. Wear simple, high-quality clothing. Do not joke excessively. In all things, carry yourself as though in the presence of the gods.

Religio and Pietas

Religio is not churchgoing. Pietas is not sentiment. Both are rooted in sacral awareness — of one's place in the cosmos, of one's duties to gods, ancestors, and tradition.

Practically: Make offerings, however simple. Light a candle to the Sun at dawn. Maintain ancestral altars. Do not let a day pass without a gesture of reverence.

The Roman did not act for applause. His strength was quiet, firm, unshakable. The Mithraic initiate likewise must eschew drama. There is no room for performative theatricality. If you must correct others, do so with calm and clarity. Move from the center; do not flail from the periphery.

To the Roman, the real was not "what works," but what endures. His realism was not base, but essentialist — focused on the spirit, gods, and natural hierarchy of things. Do not seek comforts; view suffering not as misfortune, but education. Speak without elaboration. Reject fantasy and sentimentality.

Clarity is not mere logic — it is the spiritual lucidity that allows one to see with the eye of the sun, not fog of the mob. It is an aristocratic style of thinking. Contemplate concisely, avoiding analysis unless purposeful. Be transparent in thought and deed. Strip your words and actions of ambiguity.

The Mithraic path is not mysticism, but initiatic realism. It aims not to lose the self in some vague "oneness," but crystallize the self as a solar axis between heaven and earth. Avoid cults of personality, channeling, and New Age intoxications. Do not chase altered states; instead seek lucidity, dominion, and ardor.

The Roman knew form is sacred. Boundaries are not limits, but definers of essence. The initiate honors distinctions: man and woman, sacred and profane, superior and inferior. Establish rules in life and keep them. Respect tradition and authority. Do not blur lines or be "*open-minded*," but distinct and decisive.

The Mithraic brotherhood was united not in homogeneity, but differentiation. Each man served in his role, yet was bound by a higher calling. In groups a center must be maintained. All must strengthen the whole by perfecting their part.

The Roman Style is not an ideology. It is form animated by fire; a style of being forged through solar will, ascetic mastery, and aristocratic clarity. To embody these virtues is to rise against the horizontal pull of the modern world and reestablish within oneself the Axis Mundi: the unshakable pole.

The Mithraic aspirant of today must uphold a Roman Style not because it is fashionable, but necessary. In the ruins, among the detritus of "*progress*," there remain few who choose honor over convenience and transcendence over survival.

To such men these virtues are not abstract ideals. They are weapons and armor. They are a sacred flame lighting the way back to the Primordial Tradition.

Stand upright, acting with dignity. Rise like the sun knowing Mithras Sol Invictus stands with you.

Mythopoetic Worldview

A mythopoetic worldview offers a profound antidote to an era dominated by materialism, digital abstraction, and existential ennui. Mythology can inform and inspire one's life, providing a meaningful structure to reality.

Julius Evola's Magical Idealism posits that reality is not a fixed, external construct but manifestation of the inner self. In this view, myths are symbolic representations of metaphysical truths. They serve as guides for the individual's journey toward self-realization and spiritual awakening. By engaging with myth, one grasps archetypes intent on shaping human consciousness.

Virgil's *Aeneid* exemplifies this approach. Aeneas's journey from the ruins of Troy to the founding of Rome is not just a historical or literary narrative; it is an allegory of the soul's quest for purpose and order amidst chaos. Aeneas embodies *pietas*, the Roman virtue denoting duty to the gods, family, and state. His staunch commitment to his mission reflects the path of an initiate who seeks to fulfill a higher destiny.

Macrobius' *Commentary on the Dream of Scipio* elucidates the cosmological dimensions of myth. In interpreting Cicero's text, the author presents a vision of a soul's ascent through the celestial spheres, emphasizing an importance of philosophical contemplation in achieving spiritual liberation.

In contrast to the rich symbolic tapestry of traditional myths, contemporary culture offers pseudo-mythologies such as gamification and simulation theory, complete with a concept of NPCs (non-player characters). These frameworks reduce experience to mechanistic processes, undermining the depth and complexity of being.

Gamification trivializes meaningful activities by turning them into point-scoring exercises, eroding intrinsic motivation and the pursuit of excellence. Simulation theory posits reality is an artificial construct, fostering nihilism and detachment. The NPC meme degrades life by suggesting one may lack sentience, promoting a cynical view of consciousness.

By embracing a mythopoetic worldview, one resists these and other reductive paradigms. Myths affirm personal agency, principled living, and potential for transcendence. They provide a narrative structure that imbues life with meaning, guiding individuals toward self-actualization and spiritual fulfillment.

Study works like the *Aeneid* and *Commentary on the Dream of Scipio* to internalize their symbolic meanings and moral lessons. Reflect on archetypal figures and narratives to gain insight into your own psychological and spiritual development.

Establish personal significance regarding mythic works that connect to the transcendent aspects of existence, reinforcing a commitment to the path. Challenge modern narratives that promote meaninglessness by affirming the value of purpose, tradition, and spiritual striving.

A mythopoetic worldview offers a profound alternative to the bitterness of modernity. By engaging with the symbolic richness of traditional myths, individuals can navigate the complexities of existence with purpose and clarity. This encourages a realization of one's highest potential.

Virgil's *Aeneid* is a mythopoetic blueprint for the soul's journey toward transcendence. Aeneas' peregrination from the wreckage of Troy to the origin of Rome symbolizes an initiate's path: the destruction of the old self, the trials of transformation, and the establishment of a new, spiritually aligned identity.

Aeneas's descent into the underworld serves as an allegory for the neophyte's confrontation with the subconscious and one's ancestral past. Guided by the Sibyl, he encounters shades of the dead including his father, Anchises, who reveals the future glory of Rome. This katabasis represents the necessary inward journey to attain gnosis and align with the Divine Will.

The trials faced by Aeneas — storms at sea, the temptation of Dido, warfare in Italy — mirror obstacles encountered on a passage of initiation. Each challenge demands subordination of personal desire to this highest calling, reflecting a Mithraic emphasis on discipline, courage, and fidelity.

Commentary on the Dream of Scipio offers a vision of the cosmos and a soul's journey through it. Building upon Cicero's narrative, Macrobius presents a hierarchical universe where a soul descends from the celestial spheres into the material world and must ascend back through contemplation and virtue.

The dream's cosmology aligns with the Mithraic initiatory system, which posits a seven-stage ascent through planetary spheres, each representing a level of spiritual purification. Like Scipio, an initiate must recognize the impermanence of earthly existence and a superiority of the eternal. This ascent requires the cultivation of virtues such as wisdom (*sapientia*), courage (*fortitudo*), and self-discipline (*disciplina*).

Macrobius emphasizes the importance of harmony between the microcosm (individual soul) and macrocosm (universe), a concept integral to Magical Idealism. By aligning one's inner order with the cosmic order, the initiate participates in the divine and transcends the limitations of the material world.

Evola's Magical Idealism posits reality is a manifestation of the inner self. Thus, transformation of the world begins with a change of consciousness. This philosophy aligns with a Mithraic path, where the initiate undergoes an alchemical alteration, transmuting base desires into spiritual gold.

The initiate must cultivate an unshakable center, embodying Roman virtues of *constantia* (steadfastness) and *gravitas* (dignity). This inner sovereignty reflects the Mithraic epitome of *Pater*, a spiritual father who has realized union with divinity.

The initiate outshines chaos, embodying eternal principles. By embodying the virtues of Roman tradition and engaging in the inner work prescribed by Mithraic teachings, one can reclaim the sacred path and achieve sovereignty.

Mithraic Symbolism

The Mithraic Mysteries present a rich tapestry of symbolism that encapsulates profound cosmological and spiritual truths. Moreover, the central symbols of Mithraism offer practical insights aligned with a Traditional existence.

At the heart of Mithraic iconography lies the Tauroctony, the depiction of Mithras slaying the bull. The bull may be seen as embodying raw, untamed forces of nature and desire. Mithras' act of slaying the bull signifies an initiate's conquest over base instincts, leading to spiritual enlightenment. The blood of the bull, from which life springs, represents the transformative power of sacrifice, echoing an alchemical process of turning base matter into gold.

Mithras is often associated with solar deities such as Sol Invictus, Helios, and Apollo. This association underscores his role as mediator between celestial and terrestrial realms. His identification with the sun emphasizes his function as source of light and truth by guiding spiritual awakening. The sun's daily journey across the sky mirrors a soul's path to enlightenment, with Mithras serving as prototype of this journey.

Twelve zodiacal signs are depicted surrounding the Tauroctony, signifying the cyclical nature of time and soul's journey through various stages of existence. The Mithraic

Mysteries encode astronomical knowledge, with the zodiac representing a cosmic order an initiate must comprehend to exceed. Progress through the zodiac marks a soul's ascent through planes of awareness, leading beyond spacetime.

Flanking Mithras in the Tauroctony are twin torchbearers Cautes and Cautopates. Cautes holds his torch upward, symbolizing the rising sun and a new cycle, while Cautopates holds his downward, representing a setting sun and end of a cycle. These figures embody a duality inherent in the cosmos: light and darkness, life and death, beginning and end.

The pair similarly indicate annual solar equinoxes. With his torch raised, Cautes represents the sun's passage through the north during spring. Cautopates is associated with the course of the sun along the southern hemisphere in autumn.

Another principal symbol within Mithraism is the cross formed by an intersection of celestial equator and ecliptic. This cosmic cross represents a point of equilibrium between celestial and terrestrial realms, and an Axis Mundi around which the heavens revolve. For the Mithraic initiate, this symbol serves as a focal point for meditation, aligning an individual's inner world with a greater cosmic order.

Often included in Mithraic symbology is a lion-headed (*leontocephaline*) figure entwined by a serpent and identified as the deity Aion or Chronos, representing time. This imagery holds a key to the soul's liberation from constraints of temporal existence. The lion-headed figure expresses the vicious nature of time and material world's predation — yet also its release.

To live in accord with Mithraic principles, one must internalize the symbolism presented in its mysteries. Emulate Mithras' conquest over the bull by subduing one's instincts and lower impulses through discipline and introspection. Regard zodiacal wisdom to understand one's place within our cosmic cycle, striving for coherence with patterns of the universe.

Acknowledge dual aspects of existence as signified by Cautes and Cautopates, upholding stability amid contrasting influences. Consider the intersection of terrestrial (horizontal) and celestial (vertical) paths to align personal motivation with Divine Will, advancing a fusion of microcosm and macrocosm. Seek release from the confines of time and materiality, aspiring toward eternal truths as expounded by Mithraism.

The Mithraic Mysteries highlight a journey from darkness to light, ignorance to knowledge, and internment to liberation. By engaging with these symbols not as historical artifacts but statements of truth, an initiate continues on a path toward illumination and embodiment of Mithras himself.

Mithraic Cosmology

Adherents to Roman Mithraism sought spiritual ascent through ritual initiation and celestial awareness. Central to the mysteries was a refined cosmology. This was a vision of the universe not as inert matter, but a living structure into which the soul is born and from which it must seek return.

A key to Mithraic cosmology lies in the Tauroctony: the iconic image of Mithras slaying a bull. Found in every Mithraeum (underground temple), the Tauroctony was far more than a mythic scene. It encoded an advanced astronomical and cosmological doctrine based on precession — the slow wobble of the Earth's axis causing the zodiacal backdrop of the sun's rising point at the equinoxes to change over millennia.

In this interpretation, the bull symbolizes the constellation Taurus, which was once host to the spring equinox. Mithras slaying the bull represents the sun god overpowering the Taurus age and inaugurating a new cosmic order. This corresponded to the Age of Aries, associated with Roman imperial ascendancy.

Surrounding creatures — dog, serpent, scorpion, raven, and lion — correspond to various zodiacal signs and constellations. The zodiac ring often enclosing the Tauroctony signifies the soul's imprisonment in a cycle of time and fate.

The act of slaying the bull is not brutal slaughter, but cosmic transformation. Mithras is a solar logos figure, transcending the astral fate imposed by the stars and enabling initiates to follow him toward spiritual freedom.

The twelve signs of the zodiac, frequently represented around the Tauroctony or elsewhere in Mithraic iconography, delineate not only time but also the path of the soul. In line with Orphic and Platonic cosmologies, the soul descends into the world through planetary spheres, acquiring traits and burdens associated with each level. Initiation reverses this descent: it prepares a soul to return through these domains, shedding worldly accretions and reclaiming its original divine nature.

The grades of initiation in Mithraism — such as Corax (*"Raven"*), Nymphus (*"Bride"*), Miles (*"Soldier"*), Leo (*"Lion"*), and so on — correspond to this cosmic ladder, each level raising an initiate's placement in the celestial hierarchy.

In this context, the sun is both a symbol and spiritual reality. Mithras is often shown in alliance with or as Sol Invictus (*"Unconquered Sun"*), guiding beyond mere light and shade to a higher ontological state. The initiate emulates Mithras, not merely worshipping the sun but becoming solar: radiant, sovereign, and victorious.

Mithraea were typically constructed underground, often designed to resemble caves. This is not accidental. The cave is a rich archetype across ancient Indo-European traditions, from the Platonic allegory to Zoroastrian mythology. In the Mithraic context, it represents the cosmos itself — the physical world as a womb and tomb, a place of both concealment and revelation.

According to Macrobius, a cave symbolizes the world constructed by the gods. The initiate enters this microcosmic universe, reenacts mythic deeds, and encounters symbolic death and rebirth. At the cosmic center where the celestial equator and ecliptic intersect (often symbolized by a cross or X in Mithraic iconography), the initiate experiences the still point around which all time revolves.

The ritual blade, fire, and excitement of Mithraic ritual facilitated this inward journey. Initiation was an ontological alteration of one's entire being.

Flanking Mithras in the Tauroctony are often two figures: Cautes and Cautopates, torchbearers representing the diurnal cycle and cosmic polarity. Cautes with torch raised signifies sunrise, rebirth, or ascent. His torch lowered, Cautopates denotes sunset, death, or descent.

They are dual guardians, akin to the Janus figure in Roman tradition. Their symmetry mirrors duality within the soul; eternal tension between light and dark, rise and fall. To overcome fate, the initiate must not reject one side, but integrate polarities — standing at the center between extremes.

The Mithraic cosmos was hierarchical, reflecting an Indo-European metaphysical structure. The universe was animated by divine forces, structured according to cosmic law (logos), and marked by the trials of existence. The soul, caught within the zodiacal chain, was not condemned forever, but called to rise.

The mystery rites were not didactic sermons. They were immersive, initiatic dramas revealing to a participant his place within the cosmos and potential to transcend it. Mithras as the paradigmatic conqueror models this ascent — not through passive belief but action, audacity, and sacrifice.

This mirrors Orphic and Platonic traditions. The soul must remember its divine origin, endure earthly trials, and liberate itself through gnosis and virtue. The Mithraic Mysteries, like all great mystery traditions, transformed the cosmos into a temple and life into a ritual.

Each symbol — whether the slain bull, torchbearers, or zodiacal wheel — functioned both as cosmic marker and personal mirror. The initiate was not an observer but a partaker in cosmological revealing.

Contemporary seekers can still draw from this vision. In a time when mechanistic cosmology renders the universe lifeless, Mithraism offers a sacred science and way of viewing the firmament not as chance matter, but a tapestry of realization. The soul is not doomed to waning and oblivion. It can through discipline, insight, and alignment become Mithras: one who slays time and rises like the sun.

Mithraic Initiatory Grades

Mithraism offered initiates a gradual, hierarchical path toward spiritual realization. The seven degrees corresponded to planetary spheres, each symbolizing not only a cosmological reality, but an inner transformation — a metaphysical ordeal and spiritual refinement. In Evolian terms, this is the passage in transcendence from horizontal (mastery of self in the world) to vertical (union with the supra-human).

Each degree was both symbolic and operative — representing a station of soul and a task for the initiate. The journey begins in the realm of mortality and culminates in celestial sovereignty.

1. Corax ("Raven") — Mercury — Messenger of Awakening

Symbol: The raven, sacred to Mercury, god of communication and thresholds.

Meaning: The introduction of awakening and vocation. The Corax is the neophyte who, like the raven, delivers a first message from above to the profane man within.

Challenge: Silence, obedience, and humility. Mercury governs transitions — here begins a breach with modernity, illusion, and slumber.

Application: Cultivate inner stillness and attentiveness. Accept discipline as a foundation of gnosis. The Corax must "die to the world" before he can perceive a higher call.

"All true action begins in stillness."

2. Nymphus ("Bridegroom") — Venus — Union with the Diety

Symbol: The veil. The initiate is "wedded" to Mithras.

Meaning: The stage of inner betrothal — total commitment to the path. Venus is not merely erotic, but harmonizing: the initiate must begin aligning passion with purpose, eros with will.

Challenge: Consecration and loyalty. One becomes wedded to an ideal: Mithras. Evola would describe this as a point after which the seeker becomes a *differentiated individual* — no longer pursuing outer attachment, but the transcendent within.

Application: Make the mystery your center. Reorder your life around sacred priority. Burn all bridges to mediocrity.

"Do not serve two masters. Either Mithraic Light or the abyss."

3. Miles ("Soldier") — Mars — The Warrior

Symbols: The sword and helmet.

Meaning: The initiate becomes a warrior of the spirit. This is the grade of militant resistance against modern entropy — a deliberate struggle against dark forces of the Occult War.

Challenge: Courage, discipline, and loyalty unto death. The initiate must declare war against fear, doubt, indulgence, weakness, and the false self.

Application: Physical training, combat, a record of victories and defeats (a *"Militant's Log"*). Within the *Miles* lurks always an enemy. It is this iron with which he sharpens the sword of will.

"Mithras does not abandon his soldiers."

4. Leo ("Lion") — Jupiter — Fire of Kingship

Symbol: Fire and the lion's mane.

Meaning: The Leo bears the fire of Jupiter — a symbol of spiritual sovereignty and inner nobility. Here the initiate refines strength into *dignitas*: solemnness, authority, control.

Challenge: Domination of lower nature and affirmation of inner law. The Leo acts with solar justice. He no longer obeys — he commands, within and without.

Application: Develop *constantia* ("constancy"), *virtus* ("virility"), and *sapientia* ("wisdom"). Set laws for the lower self from a higher intuition. Speak little, act decisively.

"The lion is crowned by fire."

5. Perses ("Persian") — Moon — Esoteric Knowledge

Symbol: The crescent moon, Persian garb.

Meaning: The initiate becomes one who knows the secrets. This degree signals access to a doctrinal core of the mysteries: cosmology, metaphysics, and sacred rites. In Evolian terms, this is the Magical Idealist phase.

Challenge: Mastery of symbolism, cosmology, and metaphysical law. One must now become a "custodian of tradition," not in a literal or antiquarian sense, but in the living, operative form of gnosis.

Application: Study the stellar mysteries: cosmic cycles, the zodiac, planets. Contemplate the Tauroctony, torchbearers, and celestial cross. Internalize Mithraic symbology and perceive hidden correspondences.

"He who knows the stars, knows his soul."

6. Heliodromus ("Sun-Runner") — Sun — Solar Transfiguration

Symbol: Solar rays, crown, whip, and torch.

Meaning: The Heliodromus is the Solar Warrior realized. He does not merely serve the Sun — he runs with it, bearing its fire across the world. This is the phase of transcendental action.

Challenge: To act without attachment. To shine without ego. The Heliodromus expresses the solar current through all deeds. His light burns — but leaves no ash.

Application: Practice sacred activism. Uplift others by presence, not proselytism. Embody the Roman style: clarity, dignity, and measure.

"The sun rises after the darkest night."

7. Pater ("Father") — Saturn — Lord of the Axis

Symbol: Mithras' Phrygian cap, scepter, and ring.

Meaning: The Pater is the final degree: the initiated man, crowned with spiritual sovereignty. Saturn, lord of time and death, is now transcended. The initiate becomes fixed in the eternal — unmoved in the whirlwind of the Kali Yuga.

Challenge: To reign within and radiate without. The Pater transmits the mysteries not through words, but by his being. He is both initiator and axis — a point of contact between worlds.

Application: Be the center and guide the worthy. Preserve the Rite and defend the sacred.

"Take up the dagger. Wear the crown of sovereignty. The ruins are not your tomb — they are your proving ground."

From Earth to the Stars

These degrees are not merely ceremonial — they represent a gradual de-conditioning from profane existence leading to interior renewal. In alignment with Evola's principles of hierarchy and verticality, the Mithraic grades are not about belonging to a club, but becoming something more than man.

They present a praxis of transformation deeply tied to cosmic structure. This is why the Mithraic path, though forgotten by the masses, is not dead. It remains available to the few possessing a heroic will to be; men who rise against time.

To walk this path is to walk against the current of the age. It is not for the many; it is for the aristocrats of the soul, the few who dare. Those who invoke: *Per virtutem, per ignem, per Mithram — surgo.* (*"By virtue, by fire, by Mithras — I rise."*)

Let those who would, ascend. Mithras stands with them.

The Mithraeum

The Mithraic Mysteries were centered around the figure of Mithras: god of light, truth, and solar order. As slayer of the bull, Mithras represents an archetypal warrior who transcends the cycle of birth and death through his active engagement with the forces of the world. This battle is fought not only on an external, physical plane but also within the soul of an initiate.

The Mithraeum is not merely an external place of worship but a symbol of the inner sanctum where spiritual warfare is waged. Traditionally contained within caves and subterranean sanctuaries, it reflects one's internal environment. The real temple is not an outward structure, but a sacred space within.

The Mithraeum: A Cave of Rebirth

Mithraea were built in or modeled after caves, which signified both the cosmos and a womb of rebirth. In his work *Rites and Symbols of Initiation*, Mircea Eliade emphasizes that the cave is a universal symbol of induction — a space where the initiate undergoes a transformation. The cave, dark and enclosed, mirrors the inner space of the soul where death and rebirth occur. Just as a seed must be buried in the earth to sprout, an initiate must retreat into the cave of their own inner sanctum to undergo spiritual transformation.

In Mithraism, the cave was not simply a space for physical refuge but also a symbol of the bringing clarity into the world. Just as Mithras' slaying of the bull is an act of cosmic order, the initiate's journey into the inner cave is a means of seeking stability within their own divided consciousness. The initiation process, which involved meditation, purification, and symbolic rebirth, was a means of reconnecting with this higher mandate and transcending the physical world's confines.

In contemporary practice the Mithraeum is a space dedicated to ritual. This requires the practitioner to create a sanctuary. It is to be a personal, sacred space where the battle between order and chaos can be waged.

Constructing the Sanctuary

Just as ancient Mithraic initiates would build small, symbolic temples to honor Mithras, the contemporary practitioner must also create a space (however small) to serve as refuge. This area should be dedicated to spiritual practice, devoid of distractions, and intentionally designed to foster a deep connection with the sacred. This should involve setting up an altar with a flame (candle or lamp) and dagger, preferably facing due east.

While the outer world is filled with distractions and debasing influences, the Mithraeum is a space where an initiate can retreat from the chaos of life and focus on the battle of the soul. The altar becomes a focal point for spiritual work, a place of both ritual and contemplation. The mere act of fixating upon a candle serves to reinforce one's resolve, orienting them toward the cosmic struggle ahead.

The torch, likewise, is an important symbol of light, illumination, and spiritual insight. To light a torch, whether metaphorically or literally, is to invite knowledge and clarity into one's life. Just as Mithras is associated with the light of the sun, the initiate must also seek to embody this principle of illumination in their own inner world, allowing the darkness of ignorance and confusion to be dispelled by the light of understanding and wisdom.

The dagger is also powerful symbol. In Mithraic iconography, a blade often appears as part of Mithras' attire or as a tool for ritual sacrifice. The dagger represents the initiate's will — the ability to act decisively, cut through illusion, and slay the bull of base impulses that keep an aspirant bound to the material world. In a practical sense, this might translate into a ritual of self-discipline: the act of consciously applying the will to overcome distractions, weaknesses, or vices.

Thus, the creation of a Mithraic altar — whether simple or elaborate — becomes an act of self-dedication. This altar serves as the focus of an initiate's daily ritual, the space in which they honor Mithras, invoke his energy, and commit themselves to the work of transformation.

The construction of the sanctuary goes beyond merely setting up a space; it also requires that initiates purify themselves both physically and spiritually. In the Mithraic tradition, a concept of purity was central to the initiation process. Modern practitioners must engage in similar practices of self-discipline and purification.

Many traditional initiation rites involve some form of physical purification — fasting, ablution, exposure, abstention from indulgence — as a way of preparing the body to receive higher energies. These practices are meant to strip away distractions of the material world, aligning the practitioner with a greater purpose.

In practical terms, fasting can be seen as a way of confronting the body's desires and asserting control over them. The Solar Warrior engages in a kind of combat with his own physical nature, subjugating base appetites to a higher principle of the spirit. Fasting is an expression of the warrior's will, a refusal to give in to those demands of the flesh.

Similarly, cold showers or exposure to cold are rituals of purification. The cold is symbolic of a harshness in spiritual combat, and discipline required to overcome inertia and stagnation. In present-day Mithraic practice, cold showers can be a potent way to connect with primal forces of nature, invigorating one's body and stimulating a flow of vital energy.

Finally, eschewing degenerate influences — whether excess, corruption, or distraction — is a vital aspect of purification. Mithraic spirituality is not passive but active; it requires an aspirant to actively reject forces seeking to ensnare them in base desires. This refraining can also involve detaching oneself from negative associations or settings that embolden degeneracy.

Combatting the Forces of Chaos

The Mithraic Mysteries are primarily about engaging in battle upon a plane of the spirit. An initiate is called to combat forces of chaos and entropy — whether these manifest as inner conditions, external situations, or a general decline of the world. In this battle, the initiate's primary weapon is conscious will, symbolized by the torch and dagger.

However, this war is one waged with the controlled focus of a warrior of light. The initiate must fight to maintain purity, uphold a commitment to truth, and transcend the temptations of materiality. The Mithraic path is not one of easy comfort but of continuous striving, each moment requiring vigilance and devotion.

The Mithraeum, once a physical space for initiates to come together in ritual, is now an internal fortress and a secluded space where the battle for order and transformation is waged. Through the construction of a sanctuary, purification rituals, and a firm commitment to discipline, the present-day Mithraic practitioner can embody the timeless ideals of Mithras — god of light, sacrifice, and order.

In the midst of a world in decay, the Mithraic initiate stands as a warrior who not only resists the forces of chaos but actively works to transform themselves, elevating their self and the world around them. By constructing a devoted sacred space, the initiate maintains a sanctuary permeated by the numinous, imbuing life with an *élan vital*.

Walking a Mithraic Path

This is the Kali Yuga: when the sacred has been obscured by profane; where the cosmic axis is flattened under the weight of quantity. The task of an initiate is not to flee, but overcome. It is in this spirit the Mithraic Path must be reclaimed — not as an aesthetic curiosity or arcane reenactment, but a daily form of combat, lived with the rigor and dignity of a warrior-priest.

Drawing from the profound insights of René Guénon and Julius Evola, and from the initiatic depth of Mithraism as a mystery religion oriented toward *Olympian* (noble, elevating, affirmative) transcendence, we present a practice. This is not abstraction, but application; this is not belief — it is being.

The Mithraic initiate is one who walks in fire, who looks to the sun not as a symbol but as a source, and who turns his acts into a rite — each moment as an assertion of the sacred. In an era separated from divine reality, an initial effort of spiritual rebellion is to re-align with a Solar Principle: the visible face of a metaphysical sun and logos manifest in the heavens.

The ancient Mithraists were known as *Heliodromoi* ("*runners of the sun*"). Their lives were lived in alignment with cosmic cycles, particularly the solar. The dawn was not merely a time of day, but moment of initiation repeated daily: the conquest of darkness by light.

Daily Practice: Upon waking — before all distractions or concerns of the profane world — stand facing East. Raise your right fist over your heart in the Mithraic Salute: a gesture of fidelity and solar identity.

Recite: "*Hail to the Unconquered Sun. I rise as Mithras rises. In light, in strength, in sacrifice.*"

This is ontological alignment. As Guénon emphasized, the outer act must correspond to an inner state. Your consciousness must become steady, luminous, unwavering. This daily salute is an anchor: a mark of distinction. A reminder you do not belong to this world, but act within it armed by a Higher Light.

Modernity is not merely a sociological condition — it is a spiritual disease. It is the reign of quantity, a cult of comfort, an inversion of values. Its idols are egalitarianism, consumerism, and softness. The Mithraic warrior must see these not as mere errors, but as antitraditional forces that must be fought: not politically, but existentially.

Mithraism was inherently hierarchical. It recognized spiritual grades, degrees of initiation, and a truth that not all life is equal in soul. Equality in its modern form is not justice — it is leveling. It is the obliteration of excellence; a suppression of verticality.

In your thoughts and interactions, resist the pull to "normalize" mediocrity. Refuse to reduce your standards to accommodate comfort or mass opinion. Reaffirm the natural aristocracy of spirit in all that you do.

The endless pursuit of pleasure and accumulation is the most visible mark of the man without center. The Mithraic initiate practices austerity, not out of ascetic denial, but as a mark of sovereignty. To consume less is to be more; each year, remove one unnecessary object, indulgence, or habit.

Victimhood, passivity, softness — these are the cardinal sins of a Mithraic initiate. Strength is not cruelty, but control. Virility is not arrogance, but radiant power. As Evola taught, the true man "rises above the human" by a quality of his inner stance.

Take cold showers. Discipline the body. Rise early. Move often. Avoid complaining. If tempted by comfort, say: "*This is the rite. This is my sacrifice.*"

In this struggle, modernity is not your enemy — it is your training field.

The practices above are not add-ons to daily life. They are the framework through which life is transformed into rite. The Mithraic Path is not about escaping the world, but transfiguring your place within it from passive subject to active axis.

Each day becomes a cycle of rise, combat, and reflection. Each act, however mundane, becomes a test of presence, strength, and alignment.

What Evola called the "*differentiated man*" is not a fantasy of elitism — it is living truth. He is different because his standard is invisible to the masses. He stands while others collapse, because his being exudes order in a world of chaos.

In such a life, dawn is no longer ordinary; it is theophany. This world is no longer your curse; it is your ordeal. Mythology is not fictionalized recollection; it is scripture.

And you, though hidden in the crowd, are Solar Man: secret initiate of Mithras. Bound by no dogma, guided by no institution — but by the eternal law of a higher authority.

The modern world cannot be saved, but the individual soul can be fortified. And through it a divine flame is preserved. Not for the masses or system, but a transcendent order that exists always, awaiting to be claimed.

To live the Mithraic way in modernity is to acknowledge, *"The world is unworthy — but I am not of the world. I rise, I fight, I recall. I serve no temporal lord; I am Unconquered Sun."*

Let this be your silent liturgy, your invisible armor, your daily act of revolt and recollection.

In strength. In light. In stillness.

Mithraic Induction

This ritual of affiliation is to be performed only once in earnest. It is to occur in a concealed setting (cave, cellar, or secluded natural space) echoing the *spelaeum* of an authentic Mithraeum. It *must* be performed on the 16th night of the month.

Preparation

The path of Mithras is not for the sentimental or dilettantish. It demands purification — not symbolic, but actual. The aspirant must undergo ascesis, approaching ritual not as ceremony but metaphysical ordeal. Prior to the ritual, perform these acts.

Fasting (12 hours): Fasting sharpens the will and cleanses body, purifying the inner temple. One must confront base instincts and command them to obey, for one who cannot subdue the stomach will never conquer their lesser self.

Asceticism (24 hours): The modern world assaults the senses with triviality, distraction, and lies. To depart from the mundane world is to regain poise in which sanctity dwells. This is both a deliberate withdrawal and an act of mental hygiene.

Purification: Pour a bowl of water and wash your hands, then intone, *"As water cleanses flesh, so fire purifies spirit."*

This triune preparation (body, mind, and spirit) forms the threshold. One does not step lightly across it.

Implements

Ritual Blade: Held in hand for cutting the veil as a "sword dividing illusion from vision."

Fire (Torches, Lamps, or Candles): Three sources of flame placed in the northeast, east, and southeast of the temple.

Invocation of The Torchbearers

As twin figures, Cautes and Cautopates flank the god, respectively representing an aspirant's ascent of initiatic victory and descent of initiatory hardship. Lighting the northeast then southeast fires, stand before them.

Facing their corresponding flames in turn, call upon the twins, declaring: *Cautes, qui portat lucem novi diei — praepara viam. Cautopates, custos noctis interioris — sustine animam meam in descensu.*

(Meaning: *"Cautes, who bears the light of the new day — prepare the way. Cautopates, guardian of the inner night — sustain my soul in descent."*)

These figures are both external beings and polarities of the initiate's soul. In this sense they are upward triumph and descending trial. Reconciling these is a key to dominion.

The Circle and the Cross

Stand in the center of your temple facing the east. Draw in air the Mithraic Cross formed by the intersection of vertical axis (being) as celestial equator and horizontal axis (becoming) as ecliptic. Circling it, recite: *In centro steti et circum me circulus clausus est. Ego sum medius inter caelum et terram.*

(Meaning: *"I stood in the center and a circle closed about me. I am between heaven and earth."*)

This is the Axis Mundi echoed in Macrobius' commentary on the cosmic ladder and planetary ascent. One becomes pontifex (*"bridge-maker"*) between visible and invisible.

Mithraic Invocation

Light the eastern flame and raise your ritual blade. Returning to the center and pointing it outward, the candidate begins facing north (direction of the Midnight Sun), rotating toward the fire in the east (reflecting the sun's daylight ascent).

Recite: *Deo Invicto Mithrae, lumen de lumine, vincens tenebras: adsis! Sol invictus, oculis nostris invisibilis, sed mente clara conspicuous — duce nos.*

(Meaning: *"To the unconquered god Mithras, light from light, vanquisher of darkness: be present! Unconquered Sun, invisible to our eyes yet seen with clear mind — lead us."*)

This liturgical function invokes a presence (*"praesensia"*). It is participation in the metaphysical hierarchy. Mithras has come as cosmic mediator and principle of order against chaos.

Gesture of Affiliation

Evola refers to the ritual gesture as part of a *phenomenology of dignity.* It is a spiritual bearing that reflects the reality one intends to invoke.

The Mithraic *salutatio* consists of placing the right fist over the heart, feet shoulder-width apart, spine straight. This gesture is held for 3 full breaths. Its symbolism is insightful: right hand (solar, active, directive), heart (seat of the subtle fire), upright posture (sign of verticality and immobility amid flux).

Sacrificial Contemplation

While visualizing the Tauroctony (slaying of the bull), recite: *Taurum cecidi. Vita ex morte; lux in tenebris.*

(Meaning: *"I have slain the bull. Life from death; light in darkness."*)

Consider the cosmic symbolism. The bull is chaotic vitality, telluric matter, undirected life-force. Mithras is solar will, logos, divine form. The act (*sacrificium*) is a transformation of lower into higher through force rightly dispensed: an ascesis.

Initiation is not symbolic entertainment, but *mortificatio.* It is a real metaphysical death and rebirth. The Tauroctony is an inner overcoming of base instincts by the sovereignty of spirit.

Closing Act

Raise the ritual blade — not outward, but piercing up into the skies. Recite: *Per virtutem, per ignem, per Mithram — surgo.*

(Meaning: *"By virtue, by fire, by Mithras — I rise."*)

Hold the blade steady, asserting: *Ego sum miles Solis, filius voluntatis, et stella inter tenebras.*

(Meaning: *"I am a soldier of the Sun, a son of will, and a star amid darkness."*)

Put out the flames intentionally with full exhalations. Fire extinguished by breath affirms the primacy of spirit over matter. After the rite, the inductee engages in private reflection.

This ritual is not a play, but a spiritual exercise of will and being. It is a metaphysical confrontation between the *mundus imaginalis* and a fallen world. Rites properly understood are vehicles of actualization — not enactments, but procedures.

The Mithraic Induction is a microcosmic reenactment of the great celestial drama: order triumphing over chaos, sovereignty over instinct, the Solar Hero over the bull of matter. It is not spectacle, but an unfolding of the soul.

"Take up the dagger; wear the crown of sovereignty. The ruins are not your tomb, but a proving ground."

Mithraic Ritual

It is imperative not to harbor nostalgia for the sacred, but evoke it through action. To strike against the passivity and hollowness of modernity. This links archaic mysteries with epic struggle; it is here myth becomes means and rite revolt.

Practice this ritual in the solitude of a Mithraeum. It is to be performed on Sunday following induction and repeated weekly.

Purificatio: A period of silence before the ritual. No food for two hours prior. Humble rinsing of hands with lukewarm water.

Invocation of Mithras

This call to Mithras is not supplication, but summoning. The rite begins in active presence, facing east — direction of dawn, initiation, and rebirth. Light the flame; perform the *salutatio*.

Recite: *"By Uncreated Light, by Unconquered Sun, I call upon Mithras, slayer of the bull, lord of the celestial vault. Grant me radiance to eclipse this age of iron and retrieve the lost gold."*

Lift the ritual blade skyward as a symbolic Axis Mundi piercing the heavens; then lower it toward earth, grounding the force. This is *hierophany*: a descent of transcendence into immanence. You are its container, but only if duly qualified and adequately prepared.

The Tauroctony Meditation

The bull slaying is a central theme of Mithraic myth. We recreate it not as literal act, but metaphysical conquest. The bull represents lifeforce unmastered: desire, indulgence, arrogance.

Visualization: You, as Mithras, are in a cavern of stars. Before you a great bull sits snorting and wild. You grasp it and plunge the dagger — not with animosity, but solemn reverence. From its blood, life flows; from its death, cosmos emerges.

Affirmation: "I slay the beast. I sacrifice my lesser self."

This is not metaphor, but real transformation. The act of destruction can also serve to conceive a greater form.

The path is not a line, but a spiral — a return to self at higher levels. Each grade of initiation is a conquest of territory related not to moral progress, but ontological transformation. That initiation is death and rebirth finds true expression here.

The Sacred Feast

This is not indulgence — it is sacramental embodiment. Like Mithras and Sol dining after the Tauroctony, you partake not in food, but in forces.

Elements: Bread (the solar body), wine or grape juice (the divine essence), and a beef dish (strength from sacrifice).

Before eating, recite: *"As Mithras dined with Sol, so I partake of the Sacred Feast. May this sustenance fortify my spirit."*

Ritual feasting is intentional, so eat with reverence. You are feeding spirit through flesh, not simply nourishing the body.

Closing Oath Against the Age

The ritual must not end in dissipation. It terminates with defiant poise — a return to the fallen world without being of it. You carry the Rite forward into life.

Make a final declaration: "*I stand among the ruins, yet am unbroken. The sun rises in my will; Mithras lives in my deeds. Nec spe, nec metu — without hope, without fear.*"

This is the Solar Vow: a Mithraic oath against the age. Hope is illusion and fear defeat. The Heroic Initiate proceeds not because he craves triumph; victory is in the act itself.

Extinguish the flame not with dejection, but a commanding exhale. Be assured knowing the fire burns within.

This ritual is a means of establishing a supernatural axis within a profane world. This is not a hobby, nor psychological self-help. It is warfare: spiritual, internal, and unrelenting.

The ritual is performed not to attain some aspirational state, but because the war never ends — as the sun must rise again. The Mithraist does not seek escape, but typifies sovereignty. To exist Mithraically is to live vertical and virile.

SIC ITUR AD ASTRA

("Thus, one journeys to the stars.")

Annual Celebrations

Roman Mithraism was particularly associated with the sun and its journey through the heavens. While the central image of Mithras slaying a bull (the Tauroctony) has captured the imagination of scholars, it is within the solar festivals — those marking the turning points of the solar year — that one discerns the cosmological undercurrent and metaphysical import of the cult. These festivals, though not explicitly detailed in surviving Mithraic liturgy, can be reconstructed or understood in light of astronomical iconography, Indo-European solar traditions, and the interpretive frameworks offered by contemporary scholars.

Two principal solar markers — the Winter Solstice (*Natalis Invicti*) and the Spring Equinox (symbolically linked to the Tauroctony) — form an axis upon which a Mithraic year might have pivoted. These events serve as thresholds of renewal, death, and rebirth: cosmic inflection points in the ascent.

The *Natalis Invicti* ("*Birthday of the Unconquered*") was celebrated on December 25th in late antiquity and associated with the solar deity Sol Invictus. This celebration intersected with Mithraic themes and imagery. The date marked the sun's rebirth following the longest night of the year — a time when darkness appeared to triumph only for light to begin its return.

Mithras is a cosmological deity who represents the force that orders and transcends the sphere of the fixed stars. Mithras is not the sun himself, but rather a companion and ally of the sun. He rides a solar chariot, slays the bull to enable a cosmic cycle, and participates in the metaphysical renewal of time. In this cosmological representation, the winter solstice is not merely a seasonal celebration but an expression of order being restored.

Julius Evola aligns the figure of Mithras with the Solar Hero: a firm, conquering force who embodies the principle of *virtus* and stability over telluric chaos. The sun's rebirth is thus also a reaffirmation of sovereign spirit and the divine principle within man that endures even during a dark night of the soul.

Natalis Invicti marks a symbolic victory — not only of light over darkness, but of the initiatic spark over an entropy of materiality. It is a moment that speaks to individuation of the soul: in the longest night, the initiate rediscovers an eternal flame. Mithraic initiates may have used this time for rituals of renewal or contemplation of Mithras Sol Invictus.

The Tauroctony, a central relief found in every Mithraeum, depicts Mithras slaying a cosmic bull, surrounded by zodiacal signs and planetary symbols with animal motifs (scorpion, dog, snake, raven). This act is often interpreted not as a literal sacrifice but cosmological allegory — a renewal of life through death and release of vital energies animating the world.

While the Tauroctony itself is not explicitly tied to a calendar date, scholars associate this act with springtime, particularly the vernal equinox, when day and night are once again in balance and the light begins to dominate. This astronomical event (around March 20th) aligns with Aries, first sign of the zodiac and symbol of initiation, emergence, and renewal.

Georges Dumézil, in his comparative studies of Indo-European mythology, underscores the importance of springtime renewal across initiatic warrior cults. In this light, the spring equinox could be interpreted as a moment when the Solar Warrior reenacts the cosmic slaying as a ritual of ascent.

According to Evola, a bull represents the vital forces of nature, instinct, and temporal existence. Mithras, as the transcendent agent, subdues these in order to liberate a solar essence within man. Thus, the slaying is not destruction but transmutation: a reordering of self from chaos into hierarchy, passion into power.

This vernal symbolism affirms a central theme in Mithraism: the initiate does not escape the world but masters it. The energies unleashed by the bull's death (wine, wheat, and life itself in some interpretations) suggest spiritual victory yields not ascetic withdrawal but cosmic stewardship.

Mithras derives from Mitrá (Mithra), an Indo-Iranian god of covenant and cosmic order. In the Vedic tradition, Mitrá is a deity associated with truth, oath, and investigation, upholding the *Ṛta* (cosmic law). In Zoroastrianism, Mithra is similarly a solar-judicial figure who watches over contracts and is often depicted in martial terms.

These traditions emphasize sovereignty, vigilance, and spiritual kingship. They are traits preserved in Mithras, albeit transformed through Greco-Roman influences. The Mithraic festivals are echoes of an earlier Indo-European rhythm rooted in themes of light, order, and renewal.

While historical Mithraism faded with a Christianization of the Roman Empire, elements of its solar and initiatic framework arguably survived. Christian nativity festivals near the winter solstice, an iconography of a risen sun, and motifs of heroic sacrifice and resurrection bear thematic parallels. Evola notes possible continuations of Mithraic themes in Freemasonry and "Western" esoteric systems, albeit in veiled or syncretic forms.

The solar festivals of Mithraism express a metaphysical worldview where time is not linear but cyclical, where the cosmos reflects the soul, and where mythic time is re-experienced by the initiate as personal transformation. Such rites are opportunities for the Solar Warrior to reaffirm his alignment with a higher principle. In darkness, he remembers light; in spring, he renews his oath. These cosmic moments demand not mere observance, but action: an inner act of participation in the sacred rhythm of being.

Through these hallowed observances, the Mithraic initiate does not escape into mysticism or descend into mere debauched revelry. He exists as a man of Tradition aligned vertically with the eternal, yet active within the temporal. The festivals are his reminders of *Illo Tempore*: time of the golden era.

Mithraic Fraternity

Our century is one when the sacred has retreated from public life. Our land is where gods have been exiled and the soul of the West atrophied under a weight of materialism. The Mithraic way — steeped in virility, conquest, and brotherhood — shines as an uncompromising flame in darkness. To walk this path is to assume a Traditional form, as well as personify a metaphysical stance: to stand upright in a fallen world.

This way is not for the many. It is not democratic, universalist, or exoteric. It is for the few: those called to the rigorous clarity of these Solar Mysteries. Those who recognize ascent is not collective but individual — and where renewal may happen it will be by fire, ordeal, and fidelity.

In line with a perennial metaphysical reality affirmed by both Evola and Guénon, an initiate must first understand their path is essentially solitary. A spiritual warrior (the *Miles Mithrae*) does not wait for others, nor lament an absence of a community. He embarks, walking alone against the world.

Modernity offers only collectivism or isolation — but neither in a sacred sense. The Mithraic path transcends both: it is supra-individual rather than individualist, and aristocratic rather than communal. The initiate is not a social being, but man aligned to a vertical axis of being. From this axis he draws strength — not in belonging, but from becoming.

The Mithraic adept walks in the lineage of Julian, who restored the ancient cults not to please the masses, but to re-establish order and hierarchy. Julian did not fear solitude; he reveled in it. For him, as for Evola, solitude is a natural condition of one who has surpassed the mass-man.

Do not delay your path awaiting others. Begin with discipline: rise with the sun, meditate on the mythos, study the texts of Tradition. Make your life the ritual: actions, conduct, posture must carry the seal of sanctity.

Accept that many will never understand, and that is good. Initiation is for the worthy, not servile. The man of Mithras is not alone — he is apart. His solitude is of dignity, not lack.

Yet, when destiny allows, isolated flames may find each other. Then arises the possibility of forming a *Contubernium*: a Mithraic brotherhood. This is no social club or modern group-think. It is a militant fraternity of spirit, modeled on Roman principles of honor, courage, and discipline.

In the Roman army, the *Contubernium* was the smallest unit — eight men who lived, ate, and fought together. Transposed to the spiritual realm it manifests as a brotherhood of warriors bound not by blood, but ritual.

Julian understood this deeply. His imperial court was not a mass of bureaucrats but a sacred retinue. He revived *collegia*, restored *sacra publica*, and reinitiated the mysteries — not to rebuild an empire of matter, but to reignite the soul of Rome.

Evola too recognized the importance of such discriminating camaraderie. In *Men Among the Ruins*, he speaks of the "*Order*" as a secret force: a spiritual aristocracy that does not preach, but acts, radiating strength into the formless masses. Such an Order, like the Mithraic cult, is hierarchical and discerning.

Not all who show interest are worthy. Fraternity must be earned, not offered. It is better to stand alone than be encircled by the feeble, scheming, and halfhearted.

No one is to be convinced. There is no proselytizing. Those who come must be tested — not by belief, but their capacity to discern, endure, and transform.

Speech is limited; action is emphasized. Each meeting should begin as silence, proceed with ritual, and end in discipline.

The grades of an ancient Mithraic cult — *Corax, Nymphus, Miles, Leo, Perses, Heliodromus, Pater* — are not archaic relics, but spiritual archetypes. A fraternity must reflect this order. Rank is earned through inner transformation, not declared.

Structure of a Contubernium

Pater: The spiritual head — silent, centered, kingly.

Heliodromus: The guide of rites, initiator, solar exemplar.

Miles: The disciplined soldier — obedient and strong.

Corax: The novice — silent, watching, learning.

No democracy. No consensus. Only order, function, and alignment with the Solar Logos.

Evola warns often of a danger in pseudo-initiation: forms without substance, ritual lacking transformation. True initiation must break a candidate's profane shell. It is not primarily a transmission of canon; this is an invocation of a deific presence.

The Mithraic initiations were always experiential. The initiate passed through darkness, trial, and revelation. In Mithraism, this transmission is not purely intellectual — it is ritual plus presence. The guide must possess what he seeks to transmit.

Begin with tasks, not teachings, observing responses to discomfort, correction, and stillness. Speak little — if they seek advice, impart symbols instead of instructions. Progressively introduce mythic aspects: the salutation, Tauroctony, so on.

Persistence will reveal their nature. Require a novitiate make record of their spiritual trial. Use this to indicate their quality.

To initiate is to assume karmic responsibility. Do not guide unless you are stable, upright, and clear. Otherwise you transfer not light, but confusion.

To form a Mithraic fraternity in the modern world is not merely to reclaim an ancient rite, but war against an age. It is to establish a fortress of vertical being in a world of horizontal chaos. This fraternity is not political, but it has political inferences: it undermines the false premises of our prevailing system by embodying its antithesis.

In *Men Among the Ruins*, Evola describes the task of those who resist modernity: to form centers of invisible influence, to embody principles, not propagate opinions. The *Contubernium* is one such center.

Code of Conduct

- Never advertise. Never seek followers. Be seen by those with eyes to perceive.
- Never argue. Use presence, not persuasion.
- Never relax. Discipline is not a phase — it is the bedrock of one's path.
- Your brotherhood must be a mirror of Mithras: resolute, brilliant, capable.

The Mithraic Path in the modern world is neither utopian nor nostalgic. To walk it is to choose steadfastness over comfort, ordeal over ease, command over disarray. *Contubernia* are loyal not to a time but to a principle. These are not relics of Rome — they are its essence reborn.

And to those few who come to you seeking light: offer not instruction, but a challenge. For only those who can pass through fire are worthy to bear the flame.

We are sons of the Sun, born to conquer. In strength, in the light of Mithras — we rise.

Initiatic Ascesis

"The bull is slain anew each day. The sun rises after the darkest night."

These are truths of a higher order: imperatives for an initiate who must walk a line between a visible world of dissolution and invisible realm of transcendent order. In the Kali Yuga, this final darkest age, a spiritual path does not entail reward, recognition, or ease, but ordeal. The definitive trial is ascesis itself: willed transformation of being through a crucible of inner fire.

Drawing upon the Mithraic Mysteries — where the bull is not merely slain once in mythic time, but in a daily interior struggle of the aspirant — we reveal how, in an absence of sanctified institutions, one may embody both altar and flame.

To speak of ascesis in this modern world is to speak against the world. We exist not in a spiritually conducive era, but one marked by collapse, vulgarity, hedonism, and levelling. The man among the ruins does not lament this condition; he uses it as a catalyst. For him, absence of Tradition is a challenge to become a living pillar of it.

The initiate must confront the full weight of our age: the seduction of comfort, cult of equality, and infection of nihilism. These are not cultural trends — they are metaphysical poisons seeking to erase the soul. It is not enough to resist them intellectually. One must purify their very essence of being.

This is the terrain of ascesis: a radical withdrawal not from the world as such, but from its false values. The word "ascesis" (from the Greek *askesis*) originally meant training — particularly in the martial or athletic sense. Evola returns to this root, stripping it of moralistic, monastic, or therapeutic degeneration. Ascesis is not denial for its own sake; it is integration. It is the channeling of energy upward through discipline and conquest.

In the Mithraic tradition a central rite is the Tauroctony — Mithras slaying a bull. The bull symbolizes a chaotic, instinctual, lower nature in man. But Evola insists the bull is not evil. It is sacred power that must be sacrificed, not repressed. In the slaying, that power is liberated and made to rise. This is a key to esoteric understanding: vital energies must be transmuted, not annihilated — sublimated, not inhibited.

Guénon affirms this dynamic from his own perspective. In *Initiation and Spiritual Realization*, he distinguishes between plain religious practice and true initiation: the latter involves a change in ontological state. Ascesis, then, is not a set of behaviors — it is the sacrifice of the profane self, by which the aspirant is reborn in an initiated mold. One does not "do" ascesis; it is a state of being, not a regimen.

Here lies the core of one's final ordeal. Initiation is not a one-time event, peak experience, or ritual retreat. It is *eternal recurrence*: each day the chaos of existence encroaches and it must be vanquished atop an altar of will.

The initiate must construct a daily architecture of ordeal. Not as pathology or punishment, but spiritual rhythm — an alignment of life with higher forces. Mithras is not principally a god of wisdom, but a holy warrior.

Initiation is not just symbolic — it is effective, causing a rupture in the normal state of being. The initiate becomes a different kind of man. He is no longer reactive, identified with the flux of the world, but fixed upon the axis of the Real.

He becomes an instrument of transcendence. His body, will, and actions become channels through which the unconditioned acts in the world. This is why ascesis is not escape — it is dominion. A Mithraist speaks and acts as one who radiates authority, not as one mired in the profane.

One's final ordeal is the transformation itself. To endure suffering without losing the vertical. To confront perfidy, isolation, failure without breaking alignment. This is initiation.

And when the moment of highest ordeal arrives — when a spirit feels crushed by the weight of a collapsing world — this is the hour of transfiguration. One does not flee; one does not fold. One rises inwardly, declaring: "*I slay the beast within. I stand in the ruins, unbroken. Mithras lives in my deeds.*"

Evola speaks of the Solar Man not merely as metaphor, but a real possibility. A Solar Man does not wait for things to improve, society to awaken, or structures to change. He becomes a new axis; his very being outshines the shadows.

This is an esoteric political act. The initiate, through ascesis, becomes a spiritual authority in a world of atheistic relativism. Even in obscurity, even without recognition, he holds a balance of the world within himself.

The sun rises after the darkest night, but only for those who carry this sun within. The Mithraic path is not for those seeking comfort or clarity; it is a path of fire. The final ordeal is not to be "survived" — one dies to this world reborn in spirit.

In the final ordeal, these demands reveal their true function. The Heroic Initiate marches on: upright, silent, sovereign — with the sun in his chest and blade in hand.

From Solar Warrior to Heroic Initiate

The clamor of modernity stifles a soul's upward call. Mithraism offers not a religion of consolation, but a warpath of arising. Amid ranks of the many and few — between those still immersed in the cycles of existence and those who ascend beyond them — lies a passage from Solar Warrior to Heroic Initiate. This is not a figurative shift, but metaphysical change.

The Solar Warrior is an archetype for one who lives against the current. He rejects the values of our age: a profanation of life, cult of quantity, adoration for the *last man*. A Solar Warrior is a creature of form, honor, and hierarchy — not as social roles, but spiritual realities. His battlefield is the world, his armor is inner order, his weapon is the will.

In Evolian terms, this is a man of differentiated type, what he calls an *aristocrat of the soul*. This figure embodies what may be called horizontal transcendence, not in a sense of yielding to matter, but mastering it without forsaking the physical plane. The Solar Warrior may fight in politics, art, society: anywhere form and force collide. His life becomes an arena in which Traditional values confront modern decay.

In Mithraic terms, the Solar Warrior corresponds to the grade of *Miles* ("Soldier"): those who have purified the vital forces and aligned them with the solar logos, but still operate within this terrestrial reality. They are transfigured men, but remain men. Their task is to defend sacred order, embodying the law.

Qualities of the Solar Warrior are a life ordered by inner principle, not imposed morality. He fights because he must; not because he is driven by resentment or revenge. Honor is not reputation; it is a sign of verticality within a horizontal realm. His presence exercises a centripetal force: it gathers, orders, dignifies.

This is the first level of transformation. It is necessary, but not final.

Where a Solar Warrior conquers the world, the Heroic Initiate surpasses it. He has ascended not only through action, but death — not bodily demise, but of the self as a profane entity. He has undergone a rite of transcendence not just symbolically, but ontologically. He has achieved a new plane of being.

The Heroic Initiate no longer defends the sacred; he becomes it. He is not merely radiant within time, but proceeds beyond it. This is the shift from horizontal to vertical transcendence.

This ascent through Mithraic grades culminates with Pater ("*Father*"). These are not ecclesiastical titles; they are initiatory stations. They are steps by which the soul breaks its bonds with the *human-all-too-human*, gradually assuming the mantle of a spiritual imperium. And so the Heroic Initiate is thus crowned.

Where the Solar Warrior acts in alignment with a greater force, the Heroic Initiate *is* it. He does not radiate; he emanates. He is not an exemplar within the age; he stands outside it, like Mithras himself, slaying the bull beyond space and time.

This is a realm of verticality. It is not achieved by degrees, but a qualitative leap. It is a rupture, not a progression.

He is no longer this or that; he is being itself, stilled in a human form. In a vertical ascent the final offering is one's self. He becomes the dagger and the heart. He no longer argues. His presence is command — not metaphorically, but actually.

To reach this level is to cross the solar threshold, the Helios Gate, entering the reign of Saturn: the timeless realm where Mithras feasts with Sol. This transition is a critical threshold for the Mithraic initiate. Many remain Solar Warriors — honorable, disciplined, luminous — but few make the necessary sacrifices to become Heroic Initiates.

The danger here is subtle: one may confuse outer triumph and inner poise with the culmination. Yet, the mysteries do not end with principled excellence, but metaphysical coronation.

How is this transition made? The Solar Warrior must come to a point where worldly mastery reveals its limit. No victory satisfies; no position holds. At this moment, the flame of transcendence burns out unless it finds a superior fuel.

The initiate must undergo a symbolic death. Guénon calls this *initiatic realization*: an irreversible transmutation of being. There is no technique, only readiness. As one's lesser self diminishes, a superior overtakes. The initiate's life becomes a liturgical act. He may still exist in the world, but now as one who has surpassed it.

The movement from Solar Warrior to Heroic Initiate is not linear — it is spiral, cyclic, enigmatic. The Mithraic path allows for stages, but demands totality. Practical expressions must mirror metaphysical intention.

We turn to the image of Mithras enthroned upon the celestial vault. A torch in one hand, dagger in the other, with bull slain beneath him. This is the state of the Heroic Initiate.

The Heroic Initiate becomes a spiritual sun: stable, firm, source of form. He does not descend to the world, but radiates through it. He does not speak, but commands via silence — his every breath affirms a vertical axis.

To live as Mithras is not to act as a man of light, but to be light itself. In the end, the question is not whether one knows this path, but whether one dares to walk it.

Let the flame rise. Let the bull bleed. Ascend.

Eternal Mithraic Flame

At the Roman Empire's sunset, amid encroaching shadows of spiritual decay and material excess, the cult of Mithras emerged as a beacon for those seeking transcendence. Rooted in ancient Aryan tradition and adapted to a Roman milieu, Mithraism offered initiation into cosmic alignment. In this sense it is a means of reclaiming sacrality in a profane age.

The figure of Mithras finds precursors in the original Indo-Iranian deities as gods associated with contracts, oaths, and a maintenance of cosmic order. The dual aspects of sovereignty are embodied by Mitrá (upholder of order and law) and Varuṇa (mystical and awe-inspiring aspect of kingship). This dichotomy reflects an Indo-European understanding of divine rulership as both juridical and magical — a synthesis echoing in Mithraism.

The schema of Indo-European society comprising functions of priestcraft and warfare finds expression in Mithraism's emphasis on martial virtues and cosmic power. Through a series of graded rituals the Mithraic initiate embodies these roles, ascending toward a state of spiritual sovereignty.

Mithraism's transmission into a Roman world saw the development of a mystery religion characterized by elaborate initiation rites, strict hierarchical order, and rich symbolic iconography. An account of its demography recognizes an appeal among soldiers, officers, and sovereigns — individuals drawn to its emphasis on controlled transformation.

Central to Mithraic worship was the Tauroctony: a depiction of Mithras slaying the cosmic bull. This is interpreted as a triumph of order over chaos, spirit over matter. The act, rich in astrological and cosmological significance, represents the initiate's own struggle to overcome base instincts and align with the divine order. Often constructed underground, the Mithraeum served as a symbolic womb or cave, facilitating the rebirth of an initiate into a higher state of being.

Mithraic iconography encodes a sophisticated astronomical system centered on the precession of the equinoxes. Mithras embodies a force responsible for this cosmic shift, positioning the deity as a transcendent power governing the celestial spheres. This astral dimension underscores the initiate's journey as one of cosmic ascent, mirroring a soul's progression through planetary spheres towards ultimate union with the celestial.

Such a cosmology aligns with the Mithraic grades of initiation, each corresponding to a planetary deity and representing a stage in the soul's purification and ascent. The initiate, through ritual and moral discipline, seeks to transcend the material realm, achieving a state of spiritual liberation and cosmic harmony.

Mithraism is an initiatory system aimed at awakening the transcendent self. The Mithraic rites are transformative processes facilitating a realization of the Absolute Individual.

His is a being who has actualized the divine within, standing sovereign over the material world.

Virile virtues are essential initiatory qualities. The Mithraic path is a form of Magical Idealism, wherein the practitioner actively shapes reality through inner mastery and alignment with cosmic principles. This approach rejects passive religiosity in favor of a dynamic engagement with the sacred, positioning the inductee as a co-creator of divine order.

To tread the Mithraic path requires a commitment to inner transformation. Establish a daily regimen that fosters physical, mental, and spiritual fortitude: this may include reflection, physical training, and studying sacred texts. Confront personal fears and societal pressures with steadfastness, embodying the spirit central to Mithraic initiation. Hold fast to one's duties, honoring obligations with integrity. Engage in regular contemplation of celestial order, recognizing the macrocosm's reflection within the microcosm of the self.

Mithraism offers a potent framework for spiritual realization in the modern age. By embracing its principles and practices, the contemporary seeker can transcend the material world's limitations, achieving sovereignty over self and alignment with divine order. In doing so, one rekindles the sacred flame of Mithras, illuminating a path toward eternal truth and inner liberation.

Mithraic Revival in an

Age of Collapse

To the profane, the Mysteries of Mithras are a curious historical footnote. They denote archaic debris buried beneath Christian basilicas and modern nihilism. But to the initiated these are talismans: ancient in origin, eternal in essence.

The Mithraic way is not reenactment, nor its relics museum curiosities. It is an ontological expression not of salvation, but sovereignty — personal, upright, and spiritual.

The path of Mithras is not semitic in nature. It does not include moral commandments, neurotic restrictions, or spiteful discontent. Its roots lie in a primordial Indo-European truth.

Mithras — descended from Mitra, a binding force, oath-keeper, pact-sealer — is not merely a solar deity. He is bridge between heaven and hero, cosmos and warrior. The Tauroctony is a myth of celestial dominion, of soul conquering fate.

The Mithraic initiate is not saved, but ascends. He does not confess, but overcomes — does not plead, but commands. To practice the Mithraic rite is not to "believe" but actualize. Initiation is not psychological; it is ontological.

The modern world's sickness is metaphysical, not moral. It is an absence of verticality and loss of a transcendent pole. The Mithraic rite is a willed affirmation of that axis within oneself.

Each grade of Mithraic ascent from *Corax* to *Pater* is not a symbolic role, but stage of ontic transformation. All is a test by fire. The bull slain is not a symbol of agricultural nature — it is your lesser self: passions, fears, inertia, weakness.

The dagger is not metaphor — it is the will-to-power purified by ascetic fire. The cave is not a location — it is the interior crucible of transfiguration. The sun is not distant — it is the radiant presence of sovereignty within. To practice this Rite today in the ruins of the West is to live with full awareness of our age's inversion, yet still choose ascent over regression.

The modern world is not neutral: it is a counter-initiatory machine. Every value, institution, and convenience is intended to dissolve form, upend hierarchy, and obliterate sacrality. The Mithraic Rite must be wielded like a sword on a battlefield.

The world speaks of "inclusivity" and "equality" — you swear fealty to difference and distinction. It encourages comfort and triviality — you embrace ordeal and purpose. It proclaims "progress" — you invoke a return to origins, moving through the world uncorrupted by the mire.

To persist without hope or fear is a mark of the Heroic Initiate. In a world addicted to distraction, passivity, and nihilism, the Mithraist wields primeval tools: blade, flame, will. He knows he cannot be understood by the masses — which is good. Tradition is for the few.

As Evola wrote, the true man of Tradition is "*a being standing upright in the midst of ruins.*" He wears the Mithraic crown not as an ornament, but a symbol of authority.

Stand firm, burn bright, and ascend eternal. To those who hear the call of a higher order, who feel a fire in their chest and pull of the stars above: take up your dagger and assume the crown of sovereignty. These ruins are not your tomb, but proving ground. Mithras stands among them with you.

Let this be a final invocation — uttered not in vain hope, but as affirming an abiding truth:

PER VIRTUTEM, PER IGNEM, PER MITHRAM — SURGO.

("By virtue, by fire, by Mithras — I rise.")

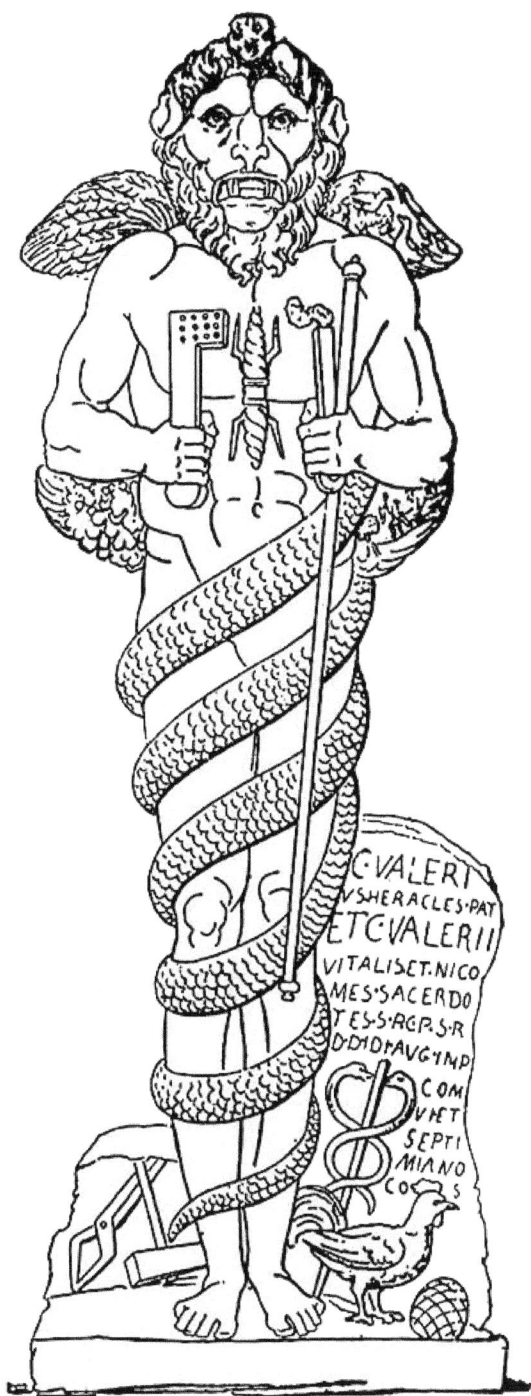

C·VALERI
V·S·HERACLES·PAT
ET·C·VALERII
VITALIS·ET·NICO
MES·SACERDO
TES·S·A·G·P·S·R
D·D·D·ID·F·AVG·IMP
COM
V·ET
SEPTI
MIANO
CO·S

www.ingramcontent.com/pod-product-compliance
Lightning Source LLC
LaVergne TN
LVHW051605080426
835510LV00020B/3133